...wright Two Vagabond Playwr...

Pitiless Storm

by

Chris Dolan

Vagabond Voices
Glasgow

© Chris Dolan 2017

First published in January 2017 by
Vagabond Voices Publishing Ltd.,
Glasgow,
Scotland.

ISBN 978-1-908251-77-0

The author's right to be identified as author of this book under the
Copyright, Designs and Patents Act 1988 has been asserted.

Printed and bound in Poland

Cover design by Mark Mechan

Typeset by Park Productions

The publisher acknowledges subsidy towards
this publication from Creative Scotland

ALBA | CHRUTHACHAIL

For further information on Vagabond Voices, see the website,
www.vagabondvoices.co.uk

Chris Dolan's Biography

Chris Dolan was born in Glasgow, graduating from that city's university in Hispanic Studies and English Literature. He became Scottish Director of Community Service Volunteers, and then International Consultant for UNESCO.

After the success of his first play, *The Veil* ("a glimpse behind the veil shows a strong future for theatre in Scotland" – *The Herald*), he decided to write full time. Chris's stage plays have been produced throughout Scotland, and in London, Milan, Spain and the USA, and have won awards including a Fringe First (Sabina 1997). He wrote the only stage adaptation of Bernhard Schlink's *The Reader* (Edinburgh Festival, 2000); he was one of the first writers to work with David MacLennan in Oran Mor – Chris eventually wrote four plays, and adapted and translated four more from Spanish for a Play, a Pie and a Pint. He wrote the libretto for the musical, *The Kist* (Edinburgh Festival 2012). In 2014 he collaborated for the first time with David Hayman in *The Pitiless Storm* for David Hayman (Edinburgh Festival and tour, 2014).

His fourth novel, *Aliyyah* is a "modern Arabian Night", examining the fault-line between atheists and theists. His third, *Potter's Field*, the first in the Maddy

Shannon mystery series, received critical acclaim when it came out in autumn 2014. *Lies of the Land* – the second in the Maddy Shannon series, came out last year. All these, plus *Redlegs* (2012) are published by Vagabond Voices. The French publishing house Editions Metaillie released a translation of *Redlegs* in 2015. They are now publishing both Maddy Shannon novels.

Dolan's first novel, *Ascension Day*, won the McKitterick Prize in 2000. His short stories have been published in newspapers, magazines and anthologies. His first collection, *Poor Angels*, was shortlisted for the Saltire Award and a story from it won the *Scotland on Sunday* prize. He was runner-up the following year. His second collection of shorts, *Hour By Hour*, came out in 2008. Dolan writes non-fiction, including *John Lennon: The Original Beatle*, and a biography of the Scottish anarchist Ethel Macdonald.

Chris has written over seventy hours of television, including *Taggart*, *River City* and *Machair*. He has written drama-documentaries, including *An Anarchist's Story* (BBC 2007). He has also written and presented TV docs including *Barbado'ed:* (BBC/Tg4; nominated for the Prix Europa), and *Don Roberto* (BBC). His films include *The Ring* (BBC), *Poor Angels*, and the Imax production, *Mistgate*.

He has written over twenty radio plays, including 2014's *The Strange Case of Dr. Hyde* (Radio Scotland) and *The House of Mercy* (Radio 4). Many of his radio plays are adaptations, including 2016's *Kidnapped*. His sixth adaptation of Ian Rankin's Rebus novels, *Fleshmarket Close*, will be broadcast later this year).

He is a regular radio and television presenter, and has written and presented over twenty hours of radio documentaries for Radios Three, Four, and Scotland. He has written audio-visual pieces for, among others, Glasgow's Transport Museum.

Chris has taught Creative Writing for many years. Currently lecturer at Glasgow Caledonian University, he was Writing Fellow, University of Strathclyde, 2011 -2012. He founded and taught at the Taller de Escritura, Pamplona, for professional writers between 2000 and 2012. He delivered master-classes for Opening Shot and Movie Makars. He ran Creative Thinking courses for BBC London and is a regular tutor at the Arvon Foundation. He has worked with writers in Brazil, Iceland, Ireland, and Italy.

He works with Creative Scotland (arts consultancy group), the Centre for Contemporary Arts, Centro Español Lorca, Robert Louis Stevenson Award, Glasgow's Aye Write, and with the NAWE Television Writing Conference.

Chris lives in Glasgow with his wife Moira Leven, while his daughter Emma works in academia in Aberdeen, and his son Daniel is finishing his medical degree in Dundee.

Preface

I had been fairly heavily involved in the public debate leading up to our Scottish Independence Referendum through public meetings and radio and TV appearances. It was a very exciting time for all of us in Scotland debating the nature of our future as a society and what its values might be. In November of 2013 when I was attending and speaking at the Radical Independence Conference in Glasgow, I was inspired by the ideas, the hope, the vision that were put forward that day from all parts of our country. So much so that while I was outside chatting to my friend Chris Dolan during a break that I blurted out, "Chris, we have to tell our story about how, as lifelong labour supporters and committed socialists we have reached the stage where we are excited about the possibility of an independent Scotland." I wanted to make a creative contribution to the debate as a performing artist, and Chris was keen to work with me on a one-man show. Together we came up with the story of a dyed-in-the-wool Labour man who goes through a crisis of conscience and ends up voting for Independence.

We talked many times over a Guinness or two, and slowly *The Pitiless Storm* took shape. It was important to me that the political message of the piece was strong and to the fore. "Let's no miss and hit the wa', Chris; we live in a very complex and unjust world, so let's hit the right targets," was my cry. Of course Chris, being the wonderful writer he is, cleverly wove the politics into a very personal and moving story about one man's journey through life and how he felt about the world and his relationships.

I performed it forty-nine times all across Scotland from Edinburgh to Inverness, from Bo'ness to Blantyre Miners' Welfare Club and from Musselburgh to a pub in Aberdeen the night before the vote. It was an extraordinary journey. I followed each performance with a discussion with the audience. Those discussions were challenging and illuminating, it was like taking a litmus test of how the people of Scotland were feeling about the choices ahead of us. I was convinced that YES were going to win by 60-40.

Each performance was a highly charged affair, we were dealing with a story that was happening, changing, evolving in the present. Bob Cunningham was talking about today, whatever day it was. It was instantly relevant, reactive to events that played out during the course of the campaign. At times the atmosphere during the performances was electrifying, with each member of the audience a highly charged particle of a greater whole. I often say that theatre is an energy exchange between an actor and an audience and it's a two-way process. We performers transmit the energy of our performance and our story to the audience, and they in turn send energy back to us in waves. The energy I sensed during those performances of *Pitiless* was quite exceptional and it took the performance to another level especially the last but one performance at Òran Mór in Glasgow. That was an extraordinary event in a packed theatre with an audience fully aware of the importance of the decision we were about to make two days hence. This was an audience that missed nothing, not a reference, not a joke, not a sub-tlety, and a highly informed and knowledgeable one on an emotional roller-coaster ride to a future none of us could predict. To me it was perfect theatre in the sense that life, art and politics all came together in one hour long monologue that reflected the excitement, confu-sion, anxiety and hope of those heady days when we discussed what kind of country we wished to be.

Needless to say I was shattered by the referendum result. That's when I again turned to Chris and said Bob Cunningham must continue. He must be a moral compass of sorts, reflecting on our turbulent times and giving voice to the frustrations and challenges that lie ahead of us in the coming years. *The Cause of Thunder* is the result. It is two years since the referendum, our world has changed dramatically and perhaps tragi-cally for the worst since then; our dreams of removing ourselves from this madness are still there and get-ting stronger. Can one old man facing retirement, Bob Cunningham, find the words and the stories to shape those dreams? I hope so, but will have to wait until February and the start of our tour before those waves of energy from my audiences give me the answer.

David Hayman, Glasgow, December 2016

Pitiless Storm

Bob enters behind the audience. He stands still for a
moment. Looks around the hall, but sees no one.
He's a little nervous, but happy, looking forward to the
evening

BOB   (*Quietly. Rubs his hands*) Yes. The big night.
   Bring 'em on.
   Been waiting for this. Ready as I'll ever be.
   How many'll be here? The loyal ones – they'll turn
   up.
   On this cold night; we must all be madmen.
   (*To Self / Young Bob*) And you… you be quiet now,
   hear?
   Leave me in peace.
   This is what I'm going to do. This is how I'm going
   to play it.
   Come in. Walk down. Say hello to a few folks.
      (*Pats his pocket for his speech*)
   Got my speech. It'll be grand.
   Okay, one last practice, before anyone gets here.

   Lights Up. Bob smiles, opens his arms in welcome

   (*To audience*)
   Good evening all! How's it going?
   Thanks everyone. Thanks for coming.
   (*Strides through audience to the stage*)
   Heeere's Bobby!
   Look at youse all.
         Jenny, alright?

Hi, Polly.
Billy ma man.
Martin, how's the aul' dutch?
Tommy – nae fighting now, hear?
Eric – wait till I get the haud o' you!
Here we all are.

He gets to the stage. Stands behind a podium.
Look at us all. Strength in numbers.
I'm looking at my life here in front of me here. My
Union. My Party. My brothers and sisters.
And this isn't my night by the way. Let's get that
clear from the get-go. This is *our* night.
We're here to look back on the road we've travelled
together. But never forgetting – we've a battle ahead
of us. A biggie. Just round the corner. But, so long
as we stick to our guns – we'll stay united and win
through.
Aren't we, all of us, without a doubt, Better thigether!

Beat

BOB   *(to younger self:)* What d'you think?
Get right into it. No self-congratulation – this isnae
about any one man. Get a feeling of camaraderie
going.
(Looks at the podium) Don't think I like this thing but.
Feel like a preacher. This isn't a party conference. It's
a party.
(Approaches the audience) No, I shall go among
my people. *(Laughs)* Like a lamb amongst wolves.
Wander back and forth a bit. Nervous energy – that's

one thing that hasn't changed. You always thought I'd grow out of that. Never did. Christ, if anything I'm worse.

(Closer) Yeah, see the whites of their eyes.

These are my people alright. Lived my whole life with them.

Ugly bastards, I'll give you that. I mean *look* at the state o' them!

Joking. They're the berries.

Okay… So here's the Plan of Action: start off with the thankyous of course. Then tell a few stories about the old days. Archie and Tommy and Polly. My dad. They all knew Da.

Will I mention Ethel? Been no word from her. Well there wouldn't be.

I was kinda hoping… Daft aul' bugger.

Maybe I won't. Mention her. No point in dredging up the past.

(Finds his notes) I've got my notes here.

Better stick to the text for this one.

BILL   *(entering)* Bob.

I'll open the doors in half an hour.

BOB   Cheers Bill.

   Beat; as Janitor Bill exits

Half an hour. And they'll open the doors.

No need to get nervous, Bobby boy. They're all friends.

Okay, this speech.

Oh man I hate *reading* speeches. That was Ethel's thing. Bloody brilliant at it she was. *(Smiles)* And then I'd get up there and go off message…
I always preferred winging it. Comes out more naturally when you do it off-the-cuff.
But this is different. Got to make sure I say the right things, in the right order.
Here goes.

(Smiles, looks up.)
Comrades… I'm overwhelmed.
(To Young Bob) Aye, "comrades". You got a problem with that? Think you own the word?

(Looks up / to audience) Comrades. I can't tell you how touched I am.
Thanks. I really mean that.
(Shows speech) See I've got it all written down. And it's no' that long. Cross my heart and hope to die. There'll be no going off on wild tangents – for once.
I'm remembering what Ethel used to say:
(As Ethel:) "Stick to your notes, Bob. And talk properly."
Mind how she used to speak, Polly? Like the Queen and La Pasionaria had been put in a blender wi' Jimmy Krankie. She was that pan-breid.
(Ethel:) "I'm reclaiming English grammar for the working class, Bob. See the cows on the pasture green; a finer sight I never have saw."
(Beat)
Well she's no' here to help me with this one.
(Beat)

Friends, this could not have come at a better time for me.

Big Six-O on the horizon. Retirement. Dicky ticker. Ethel... My Da, Bob senior, passing away. Most of you knew him. Tough in the end. You all know that. Most of you.

But I remember him as he used to be... when I was growing up.

(His Dad:) "I started oot wi' nothing' son, and I've still got maist ae it left." "Don't agonize – organize!" Fought all his days for this Party.

And the singing – (Dad singing:) "I left my fags in San Francisco..." Auld eejit, couldnae sing for toffee. (Sings:) "Bandiera rossa la triomferà..." If the old boy could see me now.

Who'd have thought it? His boy, wee Bobby Cunningham, getting an honour.

(To younger self:) You tell him. If you see him. He'll be that proud.

(Beat)

Aye he will.

(To audience:)

One of my first memories of the old man, he was outside a pub and had some poor bugger pinned up against the wall, fist pulled back, ready to give him a fourpenny one... nothing out of the ordinary in that. But he was eyeballing this poor bloke and going : (His Dad:) "I'm *tellin'* ye pal, there were five hundred and forty-*nine* Scottish volunteers in the Spanish Civil War!"

15

About to give some poor guy a hammerin' over a minor point of radical history.

(To younger self / smiles) You love all that, eh? The old man's antics.

I know, he isnae always like that. He can be a right aul' bugger, eh? Shouting at you for playing your music too loud. Bowie – man, he *hates* Bowie. Ziggy Stardust.

(Dad:) "That fella's got a make-up bag your Ma would kill for, son…. *'You pull on a finger and then another finger?'* What's that all aboot?"

But he works hard the old man. You don't appreciate that. Not yet. You'll know soon enough what he gave up for us, the price he paid. Hard times ahead, wee man.

Now, wheesht. Got to get on with this.

(Beat. Checks notes. To audience:)
The day that letter came through the post… What a fright it gave me. From the Queen? Come from my background a letter from Her Majesty's Service means the jile. MI6 must have got wind of me.

And here it was youse all along.

An OBE?

Who'd have believed it?

If someone had told me at seventeen….

(Puts up his hand to silence Young Bob)
We've grown up. All of us. Learned to live with realities.

My Dad was a realist – what's the point of shouting slogans on the sidelines, Bobby? Get in amongst 'em.

Get your hands dirty.

We're team players us. And here's me lifting the cup – on behalf of us all.

Mind you, who'd have thought it'd be an *OBE*?! Officer of the Order of the British Empire. Christ. Didn't see that coming. I had to do a bit of thinking, I don't mind saying.

It's the only system we have for recognizing achievements. You can't sit in the corner in a huff, watching all the reactionaries get the publicity. Mind fella, whatsisname, the professor. Historian. Decent guy. Made a knight of the realm, and quite right too. Working class laddie, showed he could do better than posh boys from private schools. Tells the *people's* history. So a thank-you and well done to all of us.

Even Labour politicians. There's your Neil and Glenys Kinnock a lord and a lady… *(As Kinnock:)* "We're alright! We're alright!"

Wee George Robertson – Labour Secretary of State, he's now Lord of Port Ellen. What do make of all that?

Better men than me have accepted honours.

Eh - Nelson Mandela? The Order of Merit, in 1975. And then later. 1993, George Square. I was there.

(Remembering:)
> I'm right next to him.

Well, I'm not. Closest I can get is the entrance to Queen Street station.

Probably about quarter of a mile, and five thousand people away from him.

But it's like I'm up there, with him. By his side.

Your man, Rolihlahla – that's what *his* old man cried him, "The Troublemaker"! – he's looking right at me. *Me.* Eye to eye.

(As Mandela:) "It is with humility and gratitude that I accept this scroll…"

Maybe everyone's feeling the same thing; doesnae make it any less potent. A man like that. Here. In my city. Right in front of me.

I *am* someone. I can *do* something.

(Mandela:) "I have tried not to falter; I have made missteps along the way… But I can only rest for a moment, for with freedom come responsibilities, and I dare not linger…"

If it's good enough for Madiba…

We've all worked our arses off, excuse my French. For years.

Just think…

Record levels of literacy and numeracy.

Minimum wage.

(Puts his hand up to silence Young Bob)

More nurses, doctors, police, teachers, students –

(To Young Bob) Will you keep a lid on it, son?!

Christ I remember being you: What do We Want? Fucking everything. When do we want it? Fucking Now.

You'll learn. Slowly slowly catchy monkey.

This lot know that.

Now let me get on and practice.

(Looks up; to audience:)

They were grand days, eh Tommy? Me an' you at
that Peace March in Edinburgh?

When was that again? Mind, we got into a fight!
Jeez-oh.

We were – what? – twenty? Some hooray student
starts chatting Ethel up.

I nutted him and you skelped his mate. Next thing
it's like a scene out a western, tables and chairs flying
everywhere, us knocking seven bells out of a bunch
of wanky students.

(As a younger Bob, gripping the student's collar) "This
is for pawing ma wumman, ya stuck-up fud *(headbutts
him)*..." And Tommy you goes "And this is for Cruise
missiles."

Aye well, okay, mibbe it wisnae quite like that. Some
o' they rugger buggers, Christ they can hold their
own. *(Posh boy:)* "You hold him, Hugo, while Reggie
and I give him a damn hiding."

If it wasn't for yon delegation of miners giving us
handers – we might never have got out of there alive.

That's when we first met you, Archie, eh? Barneying
at a peace march.

And then mind what Ethel said, Tommy?

(Ethel:) " I am *not* your woman, Bob. And I can fight
my own fights.

Do you lack confidence in me, Bob? Maybe you just
lack it in yourself."

(Smiles / remembering) Then she kissed me. Like
Grace Kelly kissing Cary Grant in High Noon.

I'm a lover, no' a fighter. We went home singing –
"Ground Control to Major Tom..."

I think she was proud really. That I blootered that guy.

(Beat)
Maybe no'.

(Shakes himself out of the memory. Looks up. Public smile:)
Archie - bet you wrote all the swanky words for the application form, or however this damn thing works. But I know how you *really* speak.
I must have told the rest of youse this... well you old-timers anyway ... Me and Archie were down for a miners' rally in Newcastle, Archie's home turf. We're in this working man's club playing billiards. In come some old dears and Archie, ever the gentleman, turns to the rest of us and says, dead serious *(Archie:)* "Watch the swearing now lads, there's cunt aboot."
(Smiles, shakes his head) Told that story once to Ethel. Big mistake.
(Ethel) "Archie Woods would never have used that word! You're making it up, Bob. Archie's a nice man."
(Himself) Aye, doesnae drink, doesnae smoke, makes a' his own dresses.
Don't start, Ethel. He did.
(Ethel) "Well I don't believe it. And even if it were true there's no need for you to repeat it."
(Himself) But it's important. It is, Ethel. Before we were... *(looks up:)* what do we cry it again? Reconstructed.
(Ethel) "It's *not* important, Bob. It's a story that means nothing. Of all the memories to keep, why keep that one?"
I don't know. "Cause it's funny?"

(To Young Bob:)
What age was I when I met her? Your age?
School. Year above me.
Lives up the street. Family poor as church mice. But Ethel walks about as if she's the Queen of bloody Sheba. Hand-me-downs, and every one of them make her look like Jane Fonda.
Hair halfway down her back. Wearing that paper rose in her hair. Like a Spanish señorita. Or an artist. Took violin lessons at lunchtime at school. Just a year older than me but she speaks like she's a proper woman. And that posh accent. Must be all that reading. Sylvia Plath. Steinbeck. Carrying Joni Mitchell albums. You played her Bowie: *"It's a godawful small affair, to the girl with the mousey hair…"*

She used to read out bits of James Joyce to me. Never got the hang of most of that…
…the moocow coming down the road and meeting the nicens little baby tuckoo…
But man it was magic to listen to.
(Smiles) You still finding excuses to walk past her house on the way home?
Enjoy that, kid. Great days.
And stop ogling her. That's okay for other lassies. You and your five finger love shuffle. Oh I remember.
(Beat)
Christ, Bob, come on. Get with the programme.
(Checks notes, but he's strayed too far from them.) Blah blah blah…

(To audience:) What we've achieved…

The New Deal.
(*to Young Bob*) Don't start.
(*to audience*) Two million people into work.
Paternity leave. Twenty-four days paid holiday for all workers.
(*to Young Bob / snaps*) Don't *you* quote the old man to *me*!
Don't you dare. Not Da. You have no fucking idea. No idea what's ahead of you.
(*to audience:*) Give me a minute here. Something to sort out.

(*Calmer / to Young Bob*) He's a big man in your eyes. But you haven't a scooby how life knocks the stuffing out you, son.
(*Meaner*) You want to know how it's going to be? What age are you now... he'll be fine for another, what, 20 years, working his socks off, singing his mad songs, turning out for every rally, putting posters in the windae, dancin' in the kitchen wi' ma, making you laugh, nightshifts, dayshifts, then boom.
Out of the blue. No big bolt of lightning. Me and Ethel round for tea. Ma in the kitchen. Dad's mid-sentence. Then he stops. Just looks at us. At me. And there's this weird look on his face, like he's been turned to stone. Petrified. And he struggles to say something. Takes him ages. Then he gets it out.
One word. And he can't believe it himself. He looks around as if someone else had said it.
One word.
No.
(*Beat*)

Turns out, a massive stroke.

Doesnae kill him. He's alive and kicking for another ten years. Physically fine. Far as I can tell his head's fine too. Just his speech.

(Mean / rounding on Young Bob) That's what's ahead of you son. Ten years watching the Big Man waste away. First at home till Ma kicks it. Then in shitty homes.

Gubbed. Get used to it – ten years and all he'll ever say is one word. No.

Can you imagine it? You getting the visuals? All that stuff going on in his heid, but it's just "no, no, no, no, no, no." You'll go round and visit your old man – faithfully twice, three times a week, to hear him saying - No.

No for ten fucking years.

(Bob takes a moment; settles himself)
Well this isnae helping.
(Finds his speech) What am I supposed to be saying?

(Brightens again. To audience) We've had to make decisions. All of us here.

And there's this big fight coming up.

For generations we've fought for internationalism – we're not going to give up now.

Workers of all countries unite – all that.

My Dad and his dad and Ethel and her parents, they fought against the Tartan Tories all their lives.

We've all got similar stories here, haven't we, comrades?

My Dad's mum was from a wee village in Italy.

Her Dad walked – aye *walked* – from Liguria to Lanarkshire where a cousin had an ice-cream shop. Two years later he *walked back* and got his wife and his daughter – only to go back to Lanarkshire again. Admittedly, on that third journey they only walked half the way – lazy bastards, eh? Shirkers.

Your old man, Polly, sailed underneath the cattle from Donegal. Christ, the coos had a better journey. Eric – your Polish mammy. Does she still get her words mixed up? Stopping at the "Thank and Be Restful". Aye said "hearth" instead of "heart". (*Eric's Mum:*) "You'll break my hearth, son." "I mean that from the bottom of my hearth!"

Then my old man starts singing, "I left my hearth in San Francisco…"

Some of us ended up in Glasgow, some in Manchester or Liverpool. They treated us all like shit – Gaels, Poles, Jews, Pakistanis, Irish. Then they want to create a Braveheart State? Scots Wha' Hae and all that! Give me peace.

I *told* Ethel. Christ, *her* parents – poverty-ridden Lancashire folk, a whole generation thrown away when they closed down the mills. *He* had to join the army, just to feed his weans. Gets sent to Ireland as a Black-and-friggin'-Tan fighting a war he disnae understand or believe in. Ethel's old dears birled in their graves when she started talking about Scottish Nationalism.

I told her – hold the line. Stand by your Lancashire brothers and sisters. It's a *class* war, Ethel, not a national one.

(Sending Ethel up:) "It was the *British* state that exploited us, Bob."

(Himself) "Oh and you think a Scottish one would be any different?"

(Ethel) "It could be. We could make it so."

She was wrong. That kind of talk turns us into fools. Archie, you know how I feel on this one. I've more in common with a Geordie like you, or a fella frae Manchester, a Scouser, than I have wi' a wifie frae Perth.

Strength in numbers.

We fought off the Fascists with our brothers and sisters from England, Wales, Northern Ireland.

Oh don't you worry – I know there's a long ways to go, and plenty of dragons still to fight in the United Kingdom. But they're up here as well as down there. Think of your Scottish ruling class. Wouldn't know their way down Buchanan Street.

We've got to stand firm on this one, friends.

(Beat. To Younger Bob)
You've gone a bit quiet now, lad.

We're as one on that at least, eh?

All three of us – Da, me, and my hypercritical right-on wee seventeen year-old self.

United, against the Tartan Tories.

(Beat)
Naw. Don't furrow your brow, son. Nothing to think about there.

Let me give you a lesson on life. I can do that now, cause I have lived.

Those people out there. The ones that'll be arriving

any minute – they're *your* people. Your family. Your kin. The ones you'll go through life with.

You stick by them. Solidarity.

That's what I've done. All my life. What you must do.

Aye sometimes, sometimes you don't always get what you want. Doesn't always go your way. You'll have plenty of disagreements. Arguments blazin' way into the wee small hours. But when a collective decision is made – you stick by it.

That's what this honour's for this evening. Esprit de corps. Camaraderie. Travelling the same road together. "And man tae man the world o'er…"

Janitor Bill's voice
BILL   *(off)* Ten minutes, Bob.

BOB   No probs.

Bob gathers himself again. Smiles to audience:

BOB   We're growing old, eh Archie? Polly? Start thinking of the past. *(Smiles:)* Walking
down the road mumbling to ourselves like old jakeys. Look at us … What in the name o' the wee society man *happened*?

How did I get to be this … old man.

What happened to my face? My eyes?

I look in the mirror and… I don't see it. It's just me. The way it's always been me. Then I see a photie of myself…

I was walking here tonight and I stopped to text on

my phone. And then this guy suddenly appears in front of me. Gave me a fright. An old guy. Then I realised – I was standing by a shop window. It was me. My own reflection. Didn't recognise myself. How's that possible?

Archie. Tommy. Look at youse. I see you now and I didn't even notice the changes. It's like living with someone with an illness. You don't see the deterioration. Until somebody else turns up and goes, Christ, Archie's looking old.

Polly, you're still a fine woman, but where did that... round the eyes... that... sadness... Where did it all come from?

Planet Earth is blue and there's nothing I can do....

Ethel. Wherever she is, she'll be grey now too. She'll have that sadness.

She had that anyway. Those last days we were together.

Mind that first walk we took, Ethel? You and me, up Dumgoyne. I took the paper rose out your hair and put a stem of yellow broom in its place. It was spring and the broom smelt of coconut in the sun.

It was about then you started playing the fiddle again. Oh man – you were rubbish, hen. What was that tune, over and over.... (*Sings, "Should I Fall Behind"*) "Da da da da, da da da da..." Forty times a day, the same fuckin' tune.

(*Snaps out of it / brighter*)
Sorry people. Keep going off at a tangent here. Ethel

27

would pure kill me.

(Checks notes:) Paternity leave; increased maternity leave – things my old dears fought all their lives for. Equality and Human Rights Commission! No' bad eh? On the world stage.

Scrapped Clause 28.

Record number of students in higher education.

(To Young Bob) I know! No jobs for them.

(To audience) Banned the nobs' fox hunting.

(To Young Bob) Aye okay, who cares. Fair enough. And they only banned it a wee bit.

(Turns fully to Young Bob) Why do you have to argue with me all the time?

Why can't you leave me in peace? Especially tonight.

I don't want to fall apart. Not here. Not tonight. Of all nights.

Think it's not enough that I hear my old man's voice ringing in my ears every day of the year, going No No No?

Think it's not enough that I hear Ethel? She's still inside my head an' all after all these years.

Those stories of hers I didn't want to hear. *(Ethel:)* "Once there was a warrior. With metal in his eyes. Marching. Where he set out from and where he was bound he couldn't remember. But he kept on marching, two abreast."

Two abreast? One man?! Your stories were nuts, Ethel. They really were.

Jesus my head is something else. All these stories and

noise. Put up this front to the world – good old Bob Cunningham, solid as fuck - and all time there's madness going on inside me. It's like I'm going through a nervous fucking breakdown every minute of my life. What was that thing I read – when I was your age, son. Mind?

Scottish... No, Caledonian... Caledonian Antisyzygy! That's it.

Fuck me. Can hardly even say it.

What the hell is antisyzygy??

(Listens to Young Bob a moment... Then to audience:)

That's it. That's right – "duelling polarities within a single entity."

(Laughs) That's not Just Caledonia – that's *me*. The "zigzag of contradiction" – found everywhere in Scotland and in every Scot. Who wrote that stuff again? McDiarmid? We're hauf an island. Then the Great Glen divides that half into two more halves.

Highlanders and Lowlanders. Gaelic to the west, Scots in the south, Doric in the east. Shetlandic, Orcadian and Christ knows what else. Then there's Glesga speaking a lingo they just make up as they along for the hell of it! *(Laughs)*

Oh he was right enough, yon poet mannie – we're the world's greatest bickerers. Gaels and Sassanachs, Highlander squabbling wi' Lowlander; Edinburgh and Glasgow, Kafflik and Proddie, Viking and the mad fuckin' Irish.

We could cause a fight in an empty hoose.

That's my heid. Full of wee wheels and rusty memories...

I'll be up here making this speech, and everyone'll see the same old Boaby Cunningham, doin' his stuff. And inside? Pande-bloody-monium. My Da singing the Java Jive, Ethel reciting stuff about Moocows and Baby Tuckoo. One soldier marching two abreast Playing that bloody tune – da da da da, da da da da… Ground control to Major Tom.

Christ, I'm going off my heid here.
(Beat)
Okay lets regroup. What am I saying?
I'm not here to talk about doubts.
I'm here to talk about certainties. What we *know* is right.

This is no time for doubting.
This is a time for sticking to our guns. Us and Them.
Talk about the Referendum. We're on solid ground there. That's sanctum sanctorum stuff.
I told Ethel, I told her. Told her that day…

(To audience) She insisted on going on that march. You all remember that day.
She was wrong. You all agreed.
(Appealing to audience) I mean, it wasn't black and white – sure, we all debated it till the cows came hame, didn't we? You all know that I wasnae convinced it was the right course of action. I was no Blairite – you all know that.
But he was our leader. Democratically elected.
Collectivism, mind that?
(Getting agitated) And, aye, I know he lied and Aye I

know Bush was pulling him along by his tadger, and Aye I knew he'd open the Gates of Hell and unleash the dogs of war and Aye, thousands of people would die, and Aye I was petrified by a man who thinks God tells him what to do…. Iraq was nightmare.

And Afghanistan. But what could I do?

What could any of us do? Going on a peace march against a Labour government was just downright *wrong*. You don't break rank like that. I told her that. Break rank and you're a blackleg, Ethel, a scab, a hypocrite, a defector – that's individualist politics, that's playing into the hands of the enemy. That's Tory thinking.

But oh no off Ethel goes. Wi' her placards, and that wee stupid yellow flower in her hair –at her age for chrissakes – marching next to the ladies of the west end and lib-dem students and ministers and what not. Jaysus the Ubiquitous chip must've been going slow that day. Not one of them would know what the working class even was if it jumped up and smacked them on face. They'd have shunned my old man in the street. And while Ethel's off on her frigging Peace March I go and see him in hospital going No No No non-fucking-stop and when she comes back I've made a cup of tea for her all geared up to make the peace and Ethel comes in and doesnae take of her coat and says I'm leaving.

(*Getting angry with the audience:*)
So, No, ladies and gentlemen, comrades-in-arms, I am taking your Order of the British Empire… to spite her. Ethel Cunningham née Macdonald. To

31

get it right fucking up her. Wherever she is. To spite my old man. The Great Bob Cunningham The First and his ten years o' staring me in the eye and going "Naw".

No, I'll take the bus to Buckingham Palace and shake hands wi' the Queen and, No, receive my honour on bended knee. Why the fuck shouldn't I? God knows I've earned it. "For God and Empire."

Ground Control to Major Tom – You've really made the grade....

And I'll thank everyone. All of you. *(Mock acceptance:)* I'd like to thank my mother and father – I could never have done this without your help and support. To my grandfathers and grandmothers going back fourteen generations, the Labour Party, to Keir Hardy and John McLean, dear old Ed Miliband, John Reid and George Osborne and Boris and Nigel Farage and Jack Nippy-sweetie Straw and zero hour contracts. Thank you, thank you Westminster and the Great British Commonwealth... *(angry:)* Thank you for fucking up my life and everything I stood for and what I thought it was to be a man. An O – B – fucking E.

Pause.

(To Young Bob) Happy now son?
Satisfied, Da? Ethel? Ma?
(Puts speech back in his pocket) Maybe better I say nothing, eh?
Just walk away. Before they get here.

Beat

Fact is I don't trust myself any more.
Lived the best part of my life and I don't know what any of it means. Why I said the things I said, did the things I did, took the decisions I did. *(Shakes his head)* Older and wiser? I'm lost.
I'm floating in a most peculiar way.
I'm lost, Ethel.
Da.

(To Young Bob) And I've lost you son. All those mad hopes and dreams. The things I was going to do! The man I was going to be! The new world ahead. Me and Ethel with the coconut broom in her hair...
And now... now I hear you whispering in my ear, like Satan, saying All this could be mine... *You?* Of all people? My seventeen year old self. Hissing at me, saying maybe I'm wrong. Maybe I should betray my comrades. Ethel's one thing, we all know where she stands. And we know what Da says – No. To everything.
But *you?*

I can't do it. Can't abandon everything. After all these years? My life would be a joke.
I won't do it.
(Appeals to audience:) For the love of God tell them! Tell all these mad people inside my skull, to shut the fuck up!

You want to hear it, hear what it's like? Inside *here?*

33

No. No. No.
Da da da da, da da da da
No no no Da da da
Going on and on and on, round and round in my head.

You should never have awarded me this. You started the whole thing off.

Bob hears and reacts to a litany of voices:
RECORDED VOICES
    (Ethel) Stop the war!
    (Young Bob) Block the Bomb! Scrap Trident!
(Dad) Don't agonize – organize!

Bob falls to his knees

Ground control to Major Tom. Commencing countdown, engines on…

(Ethel) And this moocow that was coming down along the road met a nicens little
boy named baby tuckoo

(Archie) Watch oot, there's cunt aboot!

(Ethel) Of all the memories to keep, why keep that one?

(Dad) No. Just say No, son. Be a man.

Da da da da da, da da da da da…

(Ethel) I need change, Bob. I'm suffocating here.

(Young Bob) Just think, old man. No nuclear weapons. No more crazy wars.

(Ethel) Why *this* piece of ground, Bob, instead of another one?

(Mandela) I have tried not to falter.

Check ignition, and may God's love be with you…

(Ethel) I am not your woman Bob

(himself) Ethel, to hear your soft voice again. I'd kneel. Plead with you.

Ten, nine, eight, ….

(Ethel) Do you lack confidence in me, Bob? Or is it yourself you don't trust?

(himself) Please god don't let me be going mad.

(Dad) There there son, no need for tears and snotters.

(Mandela) I have made missteps along the way.

Planet Earth is blue and there's nothing I can do.

Seven, six

(Young Bob) Wiznae me – you – *we* didn't kill all those soldiers and Iraqis.

(Ethel) *You* didn't put a million young people on the dole, Bob.

(Young Bob) It's no' about *being* Scottish, old man

   (Ethel) One warrior, marching two abreast.
Two armies. Across a battlefield. Gray caps, gray tunics, grey medals, mud and sand on their boots. And all the soldiers have the same face.

   (himself) And it's my face, isn't it Ethel. It's me!

   (Ethel) Up you get, Bob. On your feet.

      (himself) I've fucked it all up, Ethel. Big time. I've had it. It's over. This isn't my world any more. I'm out of here.
(He tears up his speech) Should have stuck to the speech. Like Ethel always warned.

DAD   (RECORDED)
Where you going son? Proud o' ye, Wee Man - *(Da smiles)* - and that's no' an easy thing to say for a man like me.
   You're my boy. Do what's right.

VIOLIN: STRANGERS IN THE NIGHT

BOB   *(himself)* Oh Da. Dad.

36

I never told you, but I caught you one day. You and Ma.

Popped round for a visit. You weren't expecting me. It wasn't a special night – nobody's birthday or anniversary. Not even the weekend.

I came in the kitchen, and you didn't notice me. There you were, the two of you, dressed to the nines. Ma in a long dress I'd never seen before. Her hair all tied up. Wee wisps o' grey escaping – but she looked... young. Happy.

And you in your best suit, for weddings and funerals, dickie bow, hair slicked back, the lot.

The radio was on. Sinatra. Strangers In The Night. The pair of you – dancing.

(Dances) "Love was just a glance away, a warm embracing dance away..."

Oblivious you were, to everything, apart from each other. And the dancing.

You didn't see me.

I slipped out quietly.

That was you, Da. That was my life.

Three, two. ...

BILL *(entering)* Bob? You okay?
They're here.

> Bob comes out of his reverie. Looks around, as if waking.
> Sees the audience.

BOB Oh, you're here? That the time?

37

Was in another world.
(Walking back down to stage:)
Welcome everyone. Good to see youse in the flesh.
Archie.
Polly.
Thanks everyone. Thanks for coming.
Eric.
What about ye', Tommy.
Here we all are.

When he reaches the podium:

BOB   Brothers and sisters. Sorry I'm late.
(Beat)
Why are you here? Everything I have ever believed
in, everything I've fought for is in retreat; everything
I despised and feared is on the rise.
(Beat)
So what do we do? Shake our heads and walk away,
say well, we tried?

I've done some thinking and I'm going to make a
stand. I want to thank you, profoundly, from the
bottom of my hearst... But I have to reject your offer
of an OBE.

... It's hard, isn't it, to... tease things apart. To know
which *bit* of you is talking.
Because it isn't just Bob Cunningham standing up
here talking to you.
Can't you see them? Lining up behind me... My
father, mother, my grandfather who walked from

Liguria to Lanarkshire and back *twice*. The men and women and children on the cattle boats; islanders and highlanders thrown off their land.

The miners, the shipbuilders, the steelworkers, the homeless, the immigrant, those touched by madness, the unemployed and their children and grandchildren that don't have a snowball's chance in hell, Can you no' see yourselves up here wi' us?

Standing here next to me? I've lived with you all my life. You *are* me.

Whatever I say now – and to be honest with you *I* have no idea what that's going to be yet – it's not Bob Cunningham alone talking at you. I'm just a part of us here, and where we've come from, trying to find a way home.

An occasion like this, it gets you thinking about your life. I've been talking to a lot of ghosts lately.

Many of you here knew my Missus. Ethel.

Missus. What's the right word? I don't know. Wife. Well, ex-wife. Ex-partner.

What a barren little word that is. Partner.

I long for the times when we had lovers, not partners.

I haven't the right to speak for Ethel anymore. But I can speak *about* her.

Why not *this* little piece of land, she said, rather than another one, a bigger one?

This wee piece of land makes some sense.

Without all that baggage. Trying to be a superpower, G8, G20, NATO. The weight of history, keeping Empire alive – you guys don't need me to tell you, we played our part in all that too. It wisnae a big boy that done it and ran away.

But I think we're ready to say sorry and move on.

We're no' hacking the land apart at Carlisle. Not abandoning anyone. We're no going anywhere. We'll still be here.

But *here* in this wee bit of land we could do things differently. And if it works – and surely to God we can give it a try! – then we can lead by example. Our comrades in England and Wales and Ireland. We can be an inspiration. Cause right now we're the last hope in these islands of defeating the destructive force of pitiless capital.

And we're no' leaving, they are.

It's fallen to us – in this little corner of a garden we've been given to cultivate – to keep alive the best of the Country Formerly Known as Great Britain. Stay, and everything we thought was great about it, will be gone forever. Fairness, equality, humanity. We're the last hope in these islands against the destruction of pitiless Capital.

We're not leaving. They are. We're not leaving a union, we're joining the world.

Do I have my doubts? Me? Fuck aye. I'm your man for the doubting.

None of us can tell the future. But we *do* have a damn good idea how things will turn out if we *don't* make a change. The rich'll get even richer, the poor poorer, more wars... And we'll still tread the same paths we trod generation after generation, never achieving what we set out to when we were younger and bolder.

So thank you. I know you meant well. But I cannot accept your gift.
(He picks up and tears slowly in half the OBE letter)
I won't be going to London to meet the queen. I cannot be an Officer of the Order of the British empire.

Eric, Tommy – I'm not insisting you agree with me.
We're people of independent mind. We have a responsibility to think things through for ourselves.
All I'm asking is that I'm *allowed* to think again. Reassess. And that you'll accept that change as the result of honest thought.
If you decide otherwise – I'm not going to fall out with you.
If you decide to say No, then I'll accept you've come to a different conclusion – with honesty and integrity too.

But me? I've had it up to here with No.
I want to start saying Yes again.
Yes to this place. This time. To us, here.

(Smiles) Yes to Antisyzygy. This mad wee land – of Covenanters and Catholics, Jews, Hindus, hippies, Muslims, Wee Frees, Big Frees, Middle-sized Frees, Bhuddists and schismatics and socialists – all of us argy-bargying our way through scones and Dundee marmalade. Red Clydesiders rubbing boiler-suit

41

shooders with Armani yuppies. There's even the odd Tory if you look hard enough. Pan-drop-sooking grannies black-affronted by everything they see out their windaes. Meenisters o' the Kirk, sweetie-wifies, golfers, hikers and pipers and hip-hoppers… All of us here together gie'in' it laldy, rowing and disputating to our hearts' content.

Yes, to you Ethel, wherever you are, and whoever you're with. To your paper roses and yellow broom and moocows and baby tuckoo. Ethel. Wherever you are – vaya con diós, hen. I love you. Mibbe see you along the way. I hope so because my life is full of empty spaces these days, friends. Places where lover and children and warmth and security are supposed to be. My fault. Only I can change that.

Violin: freedom come all ye

Friends. Comrades. Yes to being seventeen inside our heads. To all the mad ideas, and wild hopes. Yes to the sadness round our eyes. To the crazy man in the shop window. To all the words we've ever spoken that never go away but float in the air.

All these words swirling inside my head. Right now it's my Ma talking, and she's telling me this story: There was a mango-seller long ago, son, and he came all the way from Multan Sahiwal to the Hebridean islands. Traipsing single-track roads and knocking on doors, laden with sweet fruits and bunches of coriander.

When Ranjith speaks Punjabi now, he does it with a soft Hebridean lilt. And when he speaks the Gaelic you can hear the spice and warmth of a far-flung land.

His daughter married a man from Glasgow. The mango-seller's daughter taught the incomer Gaelic and love. And they sing ghazals in Gaelic to a bungra beat.

Welcome to my great wee Scotland. Wi' its thistles and ragged edges and uncertainties – Christ we don't even know what the weather'll be like in half an hour, let alone what the whole country'll be like in a decade.

Shaped by us with our value and our humanity.

On this cold night – we are not madmen. We're just trying to do the best we can.

We've given ourselves a wee chance. A once in a lifetime chance.

An empire of the hearth and heart.

The world's not going to fall apart. We're just taking *responsibility*.

For who we were, who we'll be – who we *can* be.

So come on. Say Aye. Sí. Oui. Da. Ya. Tha. Okay.

Just say Yes. Aye, fair do's. A'right. How no? Affirmative.

Gie' it a spin. Have a go, a crack, a shot.

Three, two, one… Yes!!

Violin tune builds and ends.

The Cause of
Thunder

by

Chris Dolan

Vagabond Voices
Glasgow

© Chris Dolan 2017

First published in January 2017 by
Vagabond Voices Publishing Ltd.,
Glasgow,
Scotland.

ISBN 978-1-908251-77-0

The author's right to be identified as author of this book under the
Copyright, Designs and Patents Act 1988 has been asserted.

Printed and bound in Poland

Cover design by Mark Mechan

Typeset by Park Productions

The publisher acknowledges subsidy towards
this publication from Creative Scotland

ALBA | CHRUTHACHAIL

For further information on Vagabond Voices, see the website,
www.vagabondvoices.co.uk

David Hayman's Biography

David Hayman was born in Glasgow and started his working life as an apprentice in a Glasgow engineering yard. After studying at the RSAMD he spent the first 10 years of his career as a founder member of the infamous Citizens Theatre Company under Giles Havergal, Philip Prouse and David Macdonald playing such roles as Hamlet, Troilus, Nijinsky, Lady Macbeth, Al Capone, Petruchio, Figaro, Bosola and, among many others, Mother Goose. At the Citz he directed *Romeo and Juliet*, his own adaptation of Thyestes, and Elizabeth!

He co-starred with Jude Law and Ruth Wilson at the Donmar in the Olivier Award winning, *Anna Christie*. He recently played King Lear in a highly acclaimed, sell-out production on his return to the Citz. His one man shows, *Six and a Tanner* and Chris Dolan's *The Pitiless Storm* played to sold-out audiences across Scotland.

He played Jimmy Boyle in *A Sense of Freedom* and followed that with over forty appearances in films such as *Hope and Glory*, *Syd and Nancy*, *The Jackal*, *Ordinary Decent Criminal*, *Vertical Limit*, *The Tailor of Panama*, *Where the Truth Lies*, *The Boy in the Striped Pajamas*, *Burke and Hare*, *Queen and Country*, *MacBeth* and

the soon to be released, *Viceroy's House*, *Dirt Road To Lafayette* and *Finding Your Feet*.

For ten years he played Detective Chief Superintendant Mike Walker in Lynda La Plante's *Trial and Retribution* for ITV. He played Jonus Franks in the BBC series *The Paradise*, Joe in *Top Boy* and Mr Turner in *London Spy*. He can be seen opposite Tom Hardy in the Ridley Scott produced TV series, *Taboo*.

David has presented many documentaries, *Clydebuilt. The Ships That Made the Commonwealth*, *Scotland's War at Sea*, *The Clyde Puffer* for BBC and *In Search of Conan Doyle*, *In Search of Burke and Hare*, *In Search of Robert Burns* and *In Search of Bible John* for STV. The STV series *On Weir's Way with David Hayman* will be followed in 2016 by *On Hayman's Way*, a six part series on Scotland. A documentary series for the BBC called *Scotch, The Story of Whisky* was transmitted in 2016.

For film, he directed *Silent Scream*, which won the BAFTA and Michael Powell Best British Film Award, as well as *The Hawk* and *The Near Room*. For TV, he directed the drama serials, *Finney*, *A Woman's Guide to Adultery*, *Cardiac Arrest* and *Firm Friends*.

For three years he was artistic director of 7.84 Theatre Company, Scotland. He directed many stage productions including the world premiers of *The Slab Boys Trilogy* and *The Normal Heart*, staring Martin Sheen. He was an associate director of the Royal Court Theatre, London.

His productions have garnered awards such as BAFTAs, Lawrence Olivier Awards, Time Out Awards, Silver Bear Award Berlin and Royal Television Awards.

He is a regular contributor to BBC 2's Review Show.

In 2001 he set up the Humanitarian Organization, Spirit Aid, which is dedicated to children whose lives have been devastated by war, poverty, disease or lack of education and opportunity. He has run the organization, as Head of Operations, since then and runs projects in Scotland, Afghanistan, South Africa, Palestine and Malawi. Spirit Aid has also worked in Guinea Bissau, Kosovo, Iraq and Sri Lanka. Once a year he visits Afghanistan and Malawi. In Scotland he created *Shooters*, a project that makes short films, dramas and documentaries with groups of young people from across the country. Almost a hundred short films have been made by over seven hundred young people from over twenty-seven different nationalities.

David has four honorary doctorates and a fellowship for services to the Arts and Humanity. He was awarded the Institute of Contemporary Scotland's Alistair Hetherington Gold Medal for Services to Humanity and was commended by the Beacon Trust for Bravery in Afghanistan. In 1991 he was given the City of Glasgow's Gold Medal for Services to the Arts.

He lives in Scotland with his wife and three sons.

Preface

I started writing *The Cause of Thunder* after a long discussion and a few pints with David at the end of 2015. I remember it being a dank, dreich night. A followup to The Pitiless Storm was always going to be very different – it was always going to be darker. Just how much darker I couldn't have guessed back then.

The first Bob Cunningham play was created during the heady days of the build-up to the Scottish referendum. Whatever side you were on the spring and summer of 2014 will be remembered as exciting, intense, dramatic. A nation discussed, argued, joked, explored. Yes there was the odd pathetic internet troll, on both sides. Undoubtedly BBC and BBC Scotland, terrified of London, messed up. But, by and large, Scotland debated passionately, wittily, and went to the polls calmly in huge numbers.

The Cause of Thunder isn't darker in tone just because the vote didn't go my way – or Bob's, or David's. Undoubtedly that's part of it – instead of Brexit we could be discussing now, with our European partners, land reform, sustainable energy, how to get rid of Trident. But so much more has happened in the last two years: President Elect Trump, Foreign Secretary Boris Johnson, the UK out of Europe, quite possibly

out of the single market, the rise of the hard right and with it the coming of the dreaded Strong Men: Putin, Erdogan, Wilders. And Strong Women: Marine Le Pen in France, Frauke Petry in Germany and Anne Coulter in the US. Then there are the attacks on minorities and the unbearable and seemingly endless tragedy of Syria... *The Cause of Thunder* could only be a more sombre, pensive affair. The death of Bowie had an odd impact – Bob had recited lines from Space Oddity throughout Pitiless, though Bowie himself was a No man. Of greater impact was the loss of a lifelong hero of mine in Leonard Cohen who died as I was writing the final drafts.

David and I met up frequently in 2015 and we discussed whether or not to do another play (in this business, you certainly wouldn't do it for the money!) and, if so, should we bring back Bob? We both liked the character. In some ways he's a little like both of us – in age, background, experience perhaps. In other ways he's nothing like either of us. In Pitiless he was so taken up with the referendum that we both felt there was more to explore in him. His obsession with his younger self, the tussle that goes on in his soul between sentimentality and political reason, his simultaneous sense of self-importance and insignificance, powerlessness. The weight of industrial city history on him. The referendum unexpectedly *not* going his way would have intensified all that. He would, I reckoned, have felt the void left by his loss of youth and, maybe most importantly of all, the absence of Ethel, his ex.

From the moment David and I started discussing this piece, from that gloomy November night in

2015, *The Cause of Thunder* began to fill itself up with loss and defeats, absences, a sense of fading light and fading strength...

The Pitiless Storm was an unusual piece of writing for me. I don't think of myself as a directly "political" writer. I had certainly never before created anything to coincide with an actual event. So this time round, working on a more ambiguous, diffuse play I felt, ironically, on firmer ground.

I can't be sure now where it came from but early on David and talked about Bob the Storyteller. We knew from Pitiless that the character could hold an audience, that he *liked* an audience. We felt that, with his friends around him, Bob would be the raconteur, the joker, the shaggy dog story-teller.

Two years ago he had very definite things to say. This time round he is as confused as the rest of us... Can we now identify a completed historical era: 1945 – 2016? What will this next era bring – some kind of vile replay of 1900 – 1945? Is the bitch who bore the bastard really in heat again? And does that mean the lives of progressive people of Bob's generation have been a waste of time? We were all wrong. Simple as that.

In the late 1990s I wrote a novel called Ascension Day. It had at its heart images of people either rising or falling. I can't say exactly why but those images came back to me when I started to recreate Bob Cunningham and the stories he might tell. The idea of Bob himself dropping down, diminishing, and rising up into the air, reminded me of a painting that I do not think I knew when I was writing Ascension Day. Stanley Spencer's Resurrection paintings, especially "Port Glasgow" had

made a big impression on me. So now three things began to mingle in my head: Bob and Ethel of Pitiless, a few "ascension" stories, and Spencer's beautiful, surprising images of people climbing out of their graves. (The fact that Ascension Day, despite winning readers, prizes, and excellent reviews was allowed to go out of print after its first run made it permissible, I felt, for me to borrow from it. That said, the stories have changed in crucial ways and in their new home with Bob they play out very differently.)

Bob's new uncertainties meant that his stories would be unsure, ambiguous. They simply occur to him and he himself wonders why. Why that particular story came to mind then and what it might mean. Where Pitiless Storm railed at the world of spin, *The Cause of Thunder* reels in the world of "post truth". Deception, racism, misogyny are now acceptable politics. The connections between things, between people, are being eroded. Bob's world has become a less anchored, more volatile and unsettling place. *Thunder*, I suspect, will be a tougher piece for audiences than *Pitiless* was. I hope, however, it will be finally at least as rewarding. It has been an exhausting, sometimes worrisome, thing to write, yet I am glad I did. (Och, and Bob is still Bob – he likes his jokes and patter!)

Working with David Hayman, apart from being a little frightening – the man simply has so much passion and energy, talent and experience – allows a writer to try things. Subtle changes of mood; the way Bob's mind – anyone's mind – hops and lurches seemingly at random from a memory to an idea, from an old story to an anxiety, from an unresolved issue to a fear of

8

the future. David can spin on a sixpence, and get the audience to spin with him. With Hayman père et fils – David junior coming along to iron out the bumps and do a final polish – you can play around with dramatic structure, with layers of meaning and effect. Theatre is the most direct form of "dreaming in public". Bob Cunningham and Ethel are the reverie, the spirits, that have come out of a deep collaboration.

The dream this time round turned out not only darker but, well, dreamier. Yet as I approached the ending I felt the writing lift, almost of its own accord. The Spencer pictures kicked in and I found myself reassessing my own old stories of ascents and descents. In part, I think, that came from working with the Haymans over two years – their commitment to their professions but also to their charitable work for Spirit Aid. This preface goes to print more than six weeks before the first performance. With nearly all the rehearsals still to come and, without a doubt, more discussions with the two Davids, the truth is I am not at all sure exactly how the play will end. I can't be sure how much of anything printed here will remain – if the early weeks of 2017 prove to be as disruptive and con-founding as 2016, Bob Cunningham will want (Bob is becoming worryingly real to me) to react to that. Still, I can't help but feel that, bad as things get, Bob is at heart a fighter and, if not quite an optimist, then some-one who rejects the binary choice between Pollyanna thinking and nihilism.

Chris Dolan, Glasgow, December 2016

The Cause of Thunder

A bar. A powerful clap of thunder.

BOB   *(off)* Blow, winds, crack your cheeks! rage! blow!

Bob almost falls in, soaked

BOB   Jesus God!!
  (Approaching audience) Ye's see that?
  Beat
  Not the storm. Bit of rain. Bit of thunder. It's winter in
  fucking Scotland for chrissakes, what' d'you expect?
  Hurricane Bawbag, every second Tuesday.
  No – *him*. That guy.
  Beat
  Nah. Ye's couldn't have.
  (Takes off coat)
  You were in here.
  The guy that rose up. Into the heavens.
  Beat.
  Aye. Right. Forget it.

  (Closer to audience)
  Fancy you lot being here.
  How youse doing?
  Been a while, eh?
  So, who's in tonight?
  Eric. Long time no see. Still got that face on you –
  like an empty hoose naebody can be arsed burgling.
  Polly, hen, a'right? Sittin' there like a repeat episode
  of Casualty.
  Sue and Billy. If you were holding hands I'd chain my
  bike to yous.

13

Looks around
Last time I was in here…
That was the night I almost got my OBE.
What a night that was, eh?
Just before the Big Day…

That was a different universe that was.
Before we were Trumped on from a great height.
Pre- post- Truth.
Mind? The world was going to change. We were going to make it change.
The Referendum.
No' that one! That last one was … just… weird.
Brexit.
Quickly followed by Regretsit; then Bremorse.
Now *there's* a story… Once upon a time there were three bold Musketeers: Athos, Porthos and Aramis.
400 years later we get the Brexiteers: Asshole, Podger, and Take-the-Piss.
Boris, Gove and Fox.
Swashbuckling heroes, led into noble battle by Sir Nigel D'ArtingTwat.
All for one and one for all? My aunt Fud. None for naebody and me for masel'.
A Brexistential fucking crisis.
How the Brex was Lost.

… Or mibbes not. In? Out? The Brexit hokey-cokey. We thought we were settled… but then we turned ourselves around.
Fuck knows what it's all about.

No. *The* Referendum. Mind? – getting the

Government we voted for. No more bombs, no more illegal wars. Justice, equality. Decency. Helping the refugee.

Being an open wee part of a Big World.

Peers at audience:

But *some* bastards voted No...

Beat

Listen. Don't let me disturb you.

Youse carry on.

I'll just sit back here. Nice and quiet.

Sits at the bar. Takes out a letter

Stuff to read. Think about.

I'll be quiet as a mouse.

Won't even know I'm here.

Pause

Thought I'd have the place to myself, right enough.

Didn't expect you lot'd be in the night. What – there nothing on the telly?

So here we all are. Back down the local. Old habits die hard, eh? Same old same old.

Sorry.

Zii-iip. Sock inserted.

Reads retirement letter. Sighs.

But really, youse should try something different. A different pub maybe. Ring the changes. Learn Portuguese. Learn to play the balalaika. Wear your knickers inside out.

It's a Trumpacious world now – nothing makes sense,

the old rules don't apply. Do whatever the fuck you want.

At least try a new drink, Polly, no? Look at youse – pint of lager, wee white wine – same pish for decades. Try a… Harvey Wallbanger why don't you? … A mint julep.

Sex on the beach. Why's it called that? Kinda promises more than it delivers, no? Might as well call it The Labour Party.

A Corbyn Sour.

Glances at retirement letter

We all need a change, not think?

I feckin' certainly do, that's for sure.

Bob Cunningham. Born Glasgow. Worked most his life for the Union. Married. Divorced. Probably die, Glasgow.

End of.

Now *there's* a short story. Christ, Solomon Grundy had a more exciting life.

My one stroke of luck, my one big moment of recognition… an OBE, an award for services to the Union and the Community – and I tell them to stuff it up their jaxies.

And for what? For a nation to collectively shite it the next day and go "Naw".

Waves retirement letter

This is the story of Bob Cunningham.

The end. That's it folks.

Clears his throat:

Gather round, children. Are we sitting comfortably? Good. Then I'll begin…

(Reads) "On behalf of the Union, I would like to

16

inform you that you are eligible for retirement in
2017."
Blah de blah de blah...
Fuck off. You're done. Over the hill. Obsolete. Last
year's man. Kaput.
Don't get my pension yet, mind. Oh no. They'll hang
on to the dosh.
I can stay if I want.... But I get the subtle impression
that they'd really rather I slung my hook. Got myself
to buggery. Piss off Bobby. Scram. Vanish. Disperse.
(Reads) "Thank you. Respectfully yours." ...
And that's the end of the story.
A fairytale ending.
And they a' died ever after.

Puts the Retirement letter down

They say it's all in the mind. Ageing.
Try telling my knees and teeth that.
You're as young as you feel – Aye, right. I couldn't
cop a feel at a geriatric orgy.
Cannae read a paper without turning to the
Obituaries. Make sure I'm still alive.
People ask me, "How are you, Bob?" And I go, "Fine.
So far as I know."
I'm a ticking bomb...

Ach listen to me. You folks came out for a good time,
and here's me all doom-and gloom.
Okay. Scout's honour. Not another word out of me.

Beat. He looks at the letter. Looks back towards the door...

That guy, though.
You ought to have seen him.
Rising up off the ground.

Sounds like a story, doesn't it.
Once upon a time there was a man. In a thunder storm….

Once upon a time,
beyond seven mountains and seven seas,
there was…
A woman. Or a man.
Who flew. Right here. Amongst us.

What happened was, I was going for the bus. Just there, the now. Saw it – the number 6 – coming up the road. So I break into a run. … You know you're old when you walk faster than you run…. Had to break back into a walk.
Missed the chuffin' bus…
But that's when I saw him.

Like he was being carried up to heaven.
Ascending.
Just past the lights there, at the park.
And he was like, walking. Walking up an invisible staircase. Like David Niven in that movie.
One foot at a time, climbing stairs that werenae there, happy as Larry.
Tap tap tap. Up he goes.
And there's me – the only direction I'm travelling is down. Six feet down and further. And I'm thinking – what the fuck?

Maybe it's the Rapture. You heard about that? True believers will be suddenly wheeched away to heaven. The End of Days.
The Good Guys, so it goes, get spirited away.
And here's me hanging about down here. Like a bad smell on a landing.
Clearly I'm not one of the Chosen.
How no'?
What, exactly, may I inquire, have I done wrong?
(Holds hand up) Aye alright, no need to give me examples. Thankyou.
I don't mean making the occasional tit of myself. Being a bit of an arsehole.
Do arseholes not get to heaven? Is that a stipulation?
You can be a Good Person, live an upright and decent life but if you're a pure numptie you're damned for all eternity?
Wankers need not apply.
That guy, stepping up the celestial ladder – what had he done that was so brilliant?
Why him? Why not me?

What do you think – was it a sign?
Was I sent a sign, some kind of… Annunciation?
You never know. … I mean, this *is* a crucial time for me.
In several ways.

Bob touches letter

Been putting this off for over a week now.
Deadline's tomorrow.

I have to decide. When I go into work. The morra.
Am I going or am I staying?
Is my life's work done?
Is that *it*?

Your man there, prancing up to the pearly gates, he
doesn't have to decide. He's been... *plucked.*

Okay, okay – I know – he didn't *actually* rise up.
It flummoxed me for a minute though, because there
he was, clearly walking upwards on thin air. A right
jaunty air to him too. Like you might have if you'd
been saved for all eternity and were going to sprout
a pair o' wings.
Bastard better have voted Yes.
But once I took a couple of steps forward I realised –
the trees in the park were obscuring my view. There
was a hill I couldn't see, right behind them.
That bloke was just walking up an ordinary hill.
It's all in the perception.
A mere mortal. Just like me, and you. Flesh and
blood, and probably – if he was anywhere near my
age – looking for a tree to pish behind.
No angels. No rapture. Just another night on this earth.

Me? I'm slowly being dragged *under* it. Like I'm sinking down... just by living, so long, my weight sinking
into the ground. Making my own grave with every
step...

Man, I'm supposed to be keeping shtum here.
Keeping my ain coonsel.

Once I start thinking of stories…
Time you get to my age, so many of them.

Beat
(smiles) Ethel was one for stories.
Things she'd remember. Things people would tell her…
I was never sure if they were true or not.
Didn't care.

Stories of the street.
Tales of cities and towns and next-door-but-one…

..,. Lying in bed. Telling each other what we'd done that day. What we thought. What we hoped for tomorrow.
And the people, the people we'd met. Stories she'd heard…

There were these two girls. Nadjme and Amber.
Best of friends they were – different families, streets, backgrounds you name it, but they were like twins.
Amber and Nadjme. Sun and the Moon.
You'd see them, walking to school, or the shop, sometimes not even saying anything, just – smiling, together.
You ever had that – someone you're so at home with you don't even need to speak? Every movement, every breath is a word. Silence is a word.
"It's like walking through a forest of whispers." That's what Amber said. That's what it felt like, when she was with Nadjme.

She'd be right there next to her, right at her side, and these... whispers would be all around, brushing their faces.

Nadjme never mentioned them. And Amber never knew where they came from or what they said, but they were always there.

At first she thought they were just the babble of passersby. But nah. These whispers only came when she was with her pal, like they belonged to Nadjme alone. Clustering round her head – singing, soothing. Saying something. Telling stories.

Angels' voices.

One day at school, Nadjme brought in a book. Amber thought it was the most beautiful thing she had ever seen. Nadjme traced her finger along the lines – the wrong way round, right to left. Speaking out the words. Words that sounded like they came from another planet, not another country.

"Yak-amár."

"Ya-rou-he."

"Habibi."

The two of them sitting on the steps of a nearby close. Keeping away from the boys, who were out looking for trouble. Having a sly fag. Searching through that book, with its lovely pictures and magical writing, looking for an angel all of their own.

"No point in looking for Christian angels", Amber said. "They'll be anti-smoking."

And then they found her.

I didn't think you got lady angels.

The Princess al'Uzzat.

One of God's watchers at the gate of heaven. She appears to us as a shooting star.

A jinnee, Nadjme called her.

"Jinnees, Bob. Jinns," Ethel told me. "There are millions of them, all around us."

A whole world of them, except they don't see us and we don't see them.

But they're here, amongst us, right now.

They're like spirits. But *they* think *we're* the spirits.

And every now and then, there's, like, a breakthrough, and humans and jinns make contact.

The writing in Nadjme's book was shapes, delicate forms that seemed to move in front of your eyes. If you looked deep enough, the words drew themselves back like a veil, and you could see all the shooting stars and shadows you wanted.

And a princess, waiting at the gate of heaven.

It was around that time – the time of the Book – that it started.

Amber began to think that, at night, when she was asleep, or half asleep, dozing, she could float out her window. Like a bird, gliding on the thermals, flying around the city at night.

Maybe she made it up – a teenage girl's daydream. Maybe she was a wee bit jealous of Nadjme's magic book.

But Nadjme believed her. And Amber told her all the wonders she witnessed at night....

Nadjme's dad opening the shop at 5 in the morning, dancing and singing and laughing to himself, out on the street, alone, in the smir, under the street lamp... The cutest boy in school. Amber swept by his tenement window fast. Deep, deep in sleep, his features calm and happy. Which pleased the girls, 'cos the boy was bullied at school where he wore a permanent frightened frown....

... *(Laughs)* Then to the teacher's house – to try and get a glimpse of exam papers!

Their teacher was still up, in the middle of the night, staring at a wall, briefcase by her side, closed.

Over the city at night she sailed. Foxes and cats, and men in the shadows, whispers whispering, lady angels, shooting stars almost within her reach.

The Princess Al Uzzat, and night flight, were better than what was happening during the day.

The trouble at school. The cat-calling. Policemen. Gangs of boys at either side of the yard, the warning whispers...

Distant roll of thunder

Amber said it was the day after the fire that she first understood what those whispers had been saying all along.

She'd dreamt she was out, coasting the night sky, sailing past her friend's house. She saw shadows there, but couldn't make them out.

Then there was a flash of light. But not a shooting star – it came from below, not above.

24

The letter bomb burnt down the door.
No-one was hurt. But Nadjme's family left the city the next day, forever.

And the whispers? ... Amber had heard the words for the first time.
They said black bastard. Paki. Fuck off, Immigrant. Darkie cunt.

Beat.

That's the story Ethel told me. That night. Lying in bed.
Couple of years later she told me she bumped into Amber.
A young woman by then.
Amber told her that, sometimes, at night, she tries to bring the dream back. She can see herself flying, high above huge mountains. If the moon is bright, or a shooting star lights up the valley for a second, she can see a house, and in the window, her friend, looking strong and healthy, sleeping peacefully.
And Amber wonders if Nadjme is dreaming about her.

Afghanistan.
Ethel saw where that war would lead before I did.
Iraq. Libya.
All the protests, the demonstrations, working for peace... all worthless.
They still bombed and killed and made millions homeless.
And now there's Syria, and Yemen. ISIS.

… Has my whole life been a waste of everybody's time?
Did I seriously get the whole thing *wrong*?
Maybe I *should* retire.
Get out of everyone's way. …
… Like I'm supposed to be getting out of *your* way.
OK. That's me done.

Sits. Looks at his letter

They've started to say to me: "That's nice."
"You out for a walk, Mr Cunningham? *'Aw, that's nice.*"
"Getting some messages in? *That's nice.*"
"Out for a wee pint? *That's nice.*"
Like I'm five, or a wee scabby dug.
If I telt them I was planning on going mental and lobbing a molotov cocktail into the United Nations headquarters they'd all go, *'aw that's nice.*"

There's a point; the tipping point. You go to the doctor's or the dentist, and they list the things wrong with you. Then they say nothing. "Learn to live with it."
You're not getting any treatment. Treatment's for young folk. No longer worth the investment.
Wear and tear.
In the good old days we just popped your clogs, didn't we?
"The Golden Age of Mortality."
The sudden, unexpected, merciful release – that's not available any more. "Passed away quietly in his bed. Surrounded by his family."

No fucking chance.

Now we keep on living, going round in circles, like a dog making its bed... day after day we're making our graves.

While smart young doctors find brilliant and fiendish ways of keeping us alive for *decades*. Brains away to buggery, tubes stuck in every orifice, one visitor a month...

Half the time I feel like I want to ... burst out greeting. What kind of a man is that?

(Posh voice:) "Come, come Bob. Let's not be an old grump, eh? Positive attitude – that's what we need! Stay young and beautiful if you want to be loved!" ... What a pile of pish, no?

I keep fit. Went to the gym last week. I stretched, pulled, pushed, jumped up and down, sweated like a pig. And that was just getting my kit on.

I keep the old brain cells going. Sudoku. All that. Crosswords.

Tell myself stories ... Which probably isn't helping. Sending me doolally quicker.

I probably don't even remember them right.

So don't believe a word I say.

What goes on, inside my head ... Voices, crazy stuff. But what goes on *out there* – walls, fences, two million children living in poverty, more and more of them every day, not less and less, kids dying, orphaned, lost, discarded...

Every one of *their* graves is another spadeful of earth out of ours.
They'll have to make our graves big enough to bury our souls as well.

Looks at his letter. But immediately jumps up, approaches audience:

"My name's Cannibal and Ah bit ma Ma's face aff!"
Barks at the audience
Stops. Pause
He didn't really. But he told people he did.

Cannibal wasn't his real name either. Stevie. He grew up in a housing estate. One of those places that voted Labour every year – and every year, unemployment grew, dampness got worse, the scheme falling slowly to pieces. Three generations of unemployed.

There was a pack of feral dogs that roamed and hunted the streets, slowly turning back into wolves and terrorizing the locals.
It was one of them that actually bit Stevie's Ma.
She got stitches. She was alright, but the scar took a long time to heal...
... And Stevie saw his chance. He told the older, tough boys – "I did that. I'm fuckin' mental!"
That kept them at bay. Gave him a wee bit peace.
The Cannibal was born.

Daffodils.
Cannibal fuckin hated daffodils.

They plant them down along the motorway. Not *in* the scheme. Not where you can touch them or anything. Up Cannibal's bit only pebbledash grows naturally.

No, they plant them in the central reservation, so if you try to get to them you get flattened by about 50 cars doing 90 miles an hour.

Huge rectangular banks of the buggers; getting their wee summery, buttery heids blown helter-skelter by buses and trucks and four-by-fours. Daft bastards.

One night – the sky like a fluorescent tube – Cannibal takes a heavy-duty drain rod to they smiley wee yellow perils.

He dodges the cars and vickies the horns and gets over to the middle of the road – between All Directions North and All Directions South...

And he kicks the shite out o' they daffies.

"Get it up ye's!"

"Aff wi' your flappy wee heids!"

He must have slaughtered over two thousand of them. Petals and stamens flying all over the joint, floating back down in shreds like confetti.

Then, knackered, he lies down in the midst of the carnage, covered in a blanket of golden dust.

That's when the Polis arrived.

They sent him to a home for mental kids in the west end of the city.

Where Ethel met him.

Suddenly Stevie wasn't the Cannibal anymore.

He was surrounded by trees and bushes and gardens –
He began to think they maybe flowers weren't such
evil bastards after all.

It wasn't their fault they were employed as border-
guards. The daffodils weren't out to get him; daisies
weren't informers. Buttercups could be quite reason-
able when approached carefully.

There was this big red tree outside his window. He
used to stare and stare at it.

"Aw right, big red tree? Don't worry – I won't batter
ye. Looks like you're bleeding already anyway."

Stevie found he was actually *good* with flowers.

He started off looking after the roses in the garden.

Then he had an idea...

Before long he was the pride of the Kids' Home.
Setting up a wee gardening business, trimming posh
folks' hedges and stuff.

He even got one of the most mental kids in the Home
to help him out.

Photofit, Cannibal christened him.

"Whit ye calling me that for?" Photofit said.

"Because, wee man," Cannibal telt him, "you he look
like several different people stuck thegether. Your
nose doesnae go wi' your eyes; your ears look like
they came off some aul' coffin-dodger. Yer arms are
long and your legs are short. Yer body looks like two
different ones glued together in the middle. Hence,
ma wee pal, you're Photofit."

"Fair do's, Cannibal."

So, they set up this wee service. RC Gardens they named their enterprise. Short for – though no one ever knew it – "Rich Cunts' Gairdens". Stevie was proud of the name.

That was when Ethel asked me to help the lads out – fair pricing, good work practice, that kinda thing. I mean, they were hardly a union shop, but I tried to give them some wee bits o' advice.

Looks like nobody needs that advice any more.
Thank you, Bob, for all your years of service. Bye now.
Away and…. What? Play golf? Winter in Tenerife and start drinking at 11AM?
Take up macramé?
What the fuck *is* macramé?
Or maybe just die. Save everybody a lot of hassle.

Anyway, that crazy pair, Cannibal and Photofit, they did well…
They specialized in planting lovely wee shrubs in driveways and window boxes.
"Mind now, Photofit – they need pruned every week."
"Ye get prunes aff them?"
"Aye very funny."
They were very – *very* – dedicated…
Nae wonder…
Soon half the detached and semi-detached houses in Poshville were home to hunners ae exquisite wee… ganja bushes.

The wee ladies were delighted. "They're absolutely gorgeous, Steven. What are they exactly? I can't find it any of my gardening books."
"It's actually a kind of weed, Missus, but it's pretty gallus, no? I call it Mary Jane."
"That's a lovely name, Steven."

Which is when the Polis arrived. Again.

Day of the hearing, Stevie was up to high doe.
And just when he'd been getting his head sorted.
Beginning to see a way he could live a life, beyond the daffodil-bordered cage he'd been born into.

He sets out up the street and after a block or two, everything goes weird.
At first he thought he was rising up off the ground.
But then he realised that wasn't it.
It was the other way round – the earth was falling away beneath his feet.
He stops dead. And it's like he's standing still but the street's being sucked down beneath him.
Then it begins plummeting away – whoosh! – under him, scaring the bejaysus out of him.
He's hanging in mid-air, terrified. Sure that any minute – like in Tom and Jerry cartoons – he's going to nosedive down, splatter himself on the ground.

Louder rumble of thunder, less distant

He can see the rooftops. The Kids' Home, the posh houses wi' their lovely wee shrubs.

That's when he works it out... Photofit had seen
Cannibal was nervous, going to his hearing.
"Have a wee tab, man. Straighten you out."
Photofit gave him a wee dose of his own medication.
Christ knows what it was.

Stevie can see almost the whole city below. The river
curling round the houses and streets.
... Red sandstone bleeding.
Beyond the city – hills, all naked and frosted.
Floating adrift like that, his body turns and twists.
He's swinging, in slow motion, till he's facing north.
Looking towards his old estate. He's surprised how
close it is to the rest of the city, to the Home and the
fancy houses.
The high rises, the grey, the empty streets. The daf-
fodils still keeping guard. The wild dogs.

The last thing Stevie the Cannibal remembers, is
shouting, into high thin air, "Ma! Mammy!!"

Pause

Stories, eh?
Half-truths.
Well, that's two I've telt you now, so that must be one
whole Truth.
Can't youse do mental arithmetic?

Maybe that's why they want me to retire.
The shite I talk.

Life's just is one P45 after another, isn't it?
Giving up childhood – to be a "man".
Cashing in your freedom, to settle down... Ethel
pensioned me off pretty fuckin' early from that par-
ticular job.
Stepping down from the five-a-sides team 'cause
your knees are knackered.
Stopping running for buses cause you can walk faster...
A series of failures, botched-jobs, defeats, capitul-
ations ...
One step after another deeper into the ground.

I'll be honest with you, guys, I'm feart.
I'm pure crapping it.
Watching friends fall like flies.
And what I'm thinking is – what's going to get *me*?

The stroke, not of luck, striking when you least
expect it.
The secret, (tender-)heart condition.
The holes being silently dug in the mind.
Cancer playing hide and seek in your body, rotting
you from inside out...

Every life ends in a horror story.
Wear and tear.

Watching my Da, say No No No, for years.
Neither up nor doon, on a flatline.
Is that what my old age is going to be, Da?
Saying No and hearing No, until the candle finally
gutters out?

Beat

I'm not supposed to talk about my Dad.
It's sentimental, apparently.
A woman told me that. I was sentimental.
About my father.
Why?
I understand less and less, the older I get, what people *mean*; why they say things.

Like people don't have strokes?
Or you're not supposed to talk about it?
Lowly beings, you see, have *sentiments*. Which are worthless.
Smarter people are logical. Rational. Higher minded.
You and me, we're *sentimental*.
… *"Aw that's nice."*

You know what? Fair do's. I can't reason anything out.
Every conclusion I come to is immediately mixed up with *feelings*.

All this stuff I have stored up here.
Years and years of stories, voices, memories, half-understood lessons.
Too stupid to make sense of any of them.
Make sense of the pain, the loss, the not-understanding…

Thunder roll; a little further back again

Ethel knew this girl once.
"She's called Paris."
"Paris? What, like a nickname?"
"No, Bob. That's what her parents christened her."
"*Why?*"
"Because she was conceived in that city."
She'd never been there herself, though. Ethel said.

There was a tree, in the street, outside Paris's window.
Somewhere not far from here.
A tree of every imaginable red.
She watched it all year, from her bed.
Reddy brown turning to browny red. Then Ruby, like a film star's lipstick. Crimson like fancy lingerie.
Paris's Dad and brother moved her bed so she could see it better.

Her mum told her over and over about the city she was named after, and Paris swore that she would see that city. She would, one day. She promised her Mum.
"I will, Mum. I swear."

A young lassie like her – *she* wasn't going to die. How could she?
They all pretended they believed it. Smiling and nodding, but Paris could see the dusk gathering in their eyes.
Dad brought her brochures. *(As her Dad:)* "Weekend breaks in the City of Love!"
"See the Eiffel Tower!"
Notre Dame and Gay Pareeee!

Paris tried not to look at her body. Scratched and torn. Inside and out.

Thing was, she *felt* strong.

It took this... blight, for her to realise her life was about the people around her.

They *were* her, and she was them.

That's what Paris told Ethel.

If she stopped existing, so would they – her mum and dad and brother, the doctors, the nurse, maybe even the strangers on the street. The mad boy selling his ganja plant everywhere.

Let the chemicals and molecules, the science, do their worst. Paris felt more alive than you could [possibly imagine

Every movement was electric. They caused her pain, but they were bolts of lightning through every part of her.

She felt – yes *felt* – *sensed* her family, her friends. They're closeness to her.

Their feelings.

Then one day she finds she's in hospital again.

No memory of having been taken there. Just Mum holding her hand and saying, "Everything's going to be fine, Love."

But when the morning came, she felt better than she had in an age.

Whatever they'd done to her, it had worked this time.

She swung her legs over the side of the bed. And

37

found she could stand, walk, easily. The power back
in her limbs.

She knew what she had to do.
Just walk home. Don't tell anyone. "Surprise, surprise! Here I am!"
Except she couldn't find her shoes.
The hospital slippers would see her up the road all
right.
Along the corridor a nurse she recognised waved to
her. "Aw right, angel?" she smiled and waved. Paris
smiled back and made for the door.

Then she's out on Dumbarton road, early morning.
Shops and shutters opening, lorries and vans, every-
thing coming to cheery life.
A new day.
It reminded her of her French school book. *Monsieur
Dupont* opening up his *boulangerie*. *Mademoiselle Verité*
cycling – en *bicyclette* – for morning coffee.
There's accordion in the air, the scent of Gaulois and
croissants.
Celui-là! Good old Glasgow's gone all *Place de la
Republique*, just for her.

Then she's at the foot of her Street, the hill that
props up her private little world. The world of family
and friends and childhood.
Up there, where the Gods live.
And she starts to climb.

Then she hears them coming.

Voices, footsteps. Chattering, skipping towards her.
Her brother, then Mum, then Dad.
Poor Mum, she's aged ten years in as many weeks.
But kick a spray of Troon sea water over her and
she'll plump up lovely. Like a Clyde Valley cherry.
Dad'll be a pushover. Just give him one of your
smiles, Paris, and next he'll be pretending he's got
something in his eye.

When they catch sight of her, they're screwing up
their eyes, hands over brows, like she's miles away.
Paris holds up her arms, and they feel young, strong,
sinewy. She waves furiously.
And now they're waving back.
Her brother punches the air. Mum's eyes wet with
tears and loving.
Above them, on the crest of the hill, her tree. Redder
than red can be. Fiery. Red-black like French wine.

Paris has never felt so light.
A sudden breeze springs up saltily from the river
below. Funnelling up the hill.
There's so little left of her that a gust hoists her right
off her feet.
There's a morning moon. Half-hidden behind a fold
of cloud. Like a young, healthy, woman's breast,
pressing against a lacy white robe.

Very distant thunder
But the tiredness comes over her again.
They'll have to catch her after all.
And they will, they will.

39

They sit round the hospital bed, pleading, "Come back Paris."
And she floats down like a feather.
And they all stand by the graveside saying, "Goodbye Paris".
Her hair wispy as a cloud, her body a gossamer, gently rocking to and fro in the air, down, down, down into arms and eyes and hearts.

Pause

I got a letter. Not this one. A while back. From Ethel. …
(Remembers:) "Bob. I'm sorry. I always meant to be in touch with you before now.
There was no anger or rejection in my silence.
I hope there wasn't in yours.
Maybe we were best not to say anything.
But I have thought about you every day, Bob, since we parted. With respect, and with a little regret.
But life takes its shape, doesn't it? We hardly seem in control of it.
We're certainly not in control of its ending.
This is not a letter I had ever imagined writing. And I have no idea how to do it…
How to say goodbye…"

I didn't know how to reply to that…
It would just have come out sentimental.

Goes to his seat
I'm not supposed to be speaking about anything.

I'm supposed to be sitting here, minding my own business. ...
... To retire or not to retire, that is the question.
Teach yourself coffin-dodging.
Croaking It Without Tears.

Sorry, sorry, sorry. I'll shut my geggie.
Let decent folk like you get on with your lives.
We'll all sit here. In the half-light.
That's me done. Finito.
Quiet as a wee moose.
I-will-Shut-The-Fuck-Up.

Pause
The thing is.
People say the last thing we need is more walls.
I agree.
"Build bridges, son", my Da used to say, "no walls."
But what do you do if the people in power are build-
ing fuckin' massive bulwarks and barriers all over the
shop? Bloody great barricades of bullying, oppres-
sion, fear...
What if your government is erecting fences to keep
out poor bloody refugees?
Bob starts pacing
Raising fences inside our heids, making us scared of
weans, feart of children who're running from guns
and war and mayhem.
And what happens behind these walls they build?
They're secretly bombing the hospitals. Killing black
folk on the streets. Shooting boys playing football on
the beach.

And everywhere there's fury. And blaming. And spite.

And now us – blaming each other. It's our fault we got it wrong. We should have seen this reactionary tide rising. We were digging our own graves all along when we spoke about racism and misogyny and hate…

Bob stumbles. Looks at his feet

Did you feel that? Something moving …

… Fury and self-righteousness; men who drink up hatred like water. Standing on podiums and hillsides like sacrilegious Sermons on the Mount. The meek, the merciful, the mourned – despised and murdered and left in the dust.

Swastikas daubed on gravestones. Murder turned into massacre, murder making money – roll up roll up, the younger you kill 'em the more profit you fucking make!

Beat. Calmer:

If you have to build one wee wall to keep out all of that Hell, well maybe you should.

A nice wee wall. Wee dry-stane-dyke-type wall.

But nah. We don't need a wall.

We're for making doors.

Come awa' ben. Wherever you're from. Whatever they've done to you. You're at your auntie's.

Ethel knew all that. What we had to do.

Long before I did.

But now I'm old and there's no Ethel and nothing I've ever done means *anything*.

And all these voices inside my head:

Me at sixteen: *(Young Bob:)* "What happened to 'I hope I die before I get old' and all that?!"

Yeah, well... Never thought I actually *would* grow old.

(Young Bob:) "Jeez, you Baby Boomers got the lot, didn't you? Cheap houses, cheap beer. Cheap education – Christ, not only was it free, they gave you fucking grants!"

Hang on there, boy. Wasn't "free" – we just had a decent taxing system.

(His Dad:) "My generation created that world for you, son."

Oh great. Inside my head, my old Dad and my younger self ganging up on me.

Pacing:

(His Dad:) "We lived through the Depression, the War, rationing. We created the Welfare State for you. The NHS. And your lot piss it all up against the wall."

(Young Bob:) "Young folk can't get jobs. Houses. Loans. While you old farts go on foreign holidays and cruises, then come home and drain the NHS dry with your strokes, living 20 years longer than you need to. Your gold-plated pensions bankrupting the rest of us – we're paid a pittance, on zero-hour contracts, to sit by your beds and wipe your slavers and arses!"

(Beat. Young Bob continues:) "Jesus – how did I get to be *you*?!"

(His Dad:) "You failed, son – everything we stood for is in freefall. Everything we battled against, on the rise. How did you let that happen?"

(Young Bob / sneers:) "Do I really end up like *you*?"
Distant thunder
(Taps his head) You were so fucking sure of yourself back then! You were going to save the world! Sixteen years old, Che Guevara and Jesus Christ and Nelson Mandela rolled into one.

Yes, *I* am what you became.

Watching Afghanistan, Iraq, Libya, Syria burn...

Millionaires and entertainers getting gongs from the queen while nurses' wages are capped.

And now listening to the casualties of a rotten system thinking they're kicking the establishment.

Well, fuck's sake, what did we *expect*?! ... If you've got a shit job and a shit house, or no job and no house, you're not going to vote for the status quo, are you? *Any* kind of fucking change can only be for the better.

We never gave anyone a better option.
Thunder closer
We're watching the planet slowly die. Floods and forest fires and famines. The whole earth going up in smoke or washed down the drain while the money-men talk about oil prices. Wars over pipelines.

Wars over water. What next – the air we breathe?

And what do we do?

Blame the immigrant.

Believe the lie that the men who bled most from the establishment – the millionaires, crooks, brokers, traders, gutter press hacks are somehow *anti*-establishment! Christ, they can't believe they're getting away with it. Time to throw up a dictator or two.

Lets go for it. Let the fun begin. The blaming and maiming, the division and killing. Let's bring the good old days back!

(*Firebrand minister:*) "The unbelieving, the vile, the murderers, the immoral, the necromancers, the idolaters and all liars – all will be consigned to the fiery lake of burning sulphur. For this is the second death!"

Thunder closer still

And where does that come from? The thunder.
Nature drumming her fingers; at her wits end.
God's dying words.
The earth about to turn itself inside out...
Spit, fire! spout, rain!
Let fall your horrible pleasure on
A poor, weak, despised old man:

I'm not just falling here, Ethel, I'm being sucked under. Down into darkness. Like some beast, below the ground, is reaching up, pulling me down, down, down.

Stumbles again. Looks down.
Can you feel it? The ground giving way beneath us.
Time for one last story...

Once upon a time.
The other night.
On the telly.
Beyond seven mountains and seven seas, there was...
An old man. Like me.
Around him there were lines of people.

This was on the telly.

Exhausted people. Scores of them. Soaked, frightened, washed up on some beach in a foreign country. And among them, a family. A wee boy. His Ma was too done in, too confused to lift him when he cried. The wean just lying there on the sand.

But then this man comes over. A local. I dunno, maybe a volunteer or something.

He'd be about my age, in a different country, with a different language – but Me, another version of Me, in a different world.

That's what Paris said – she *was* her mum, her dad, her brother, and they were her.

And *we're* all that wean, lying on the sand. We're all his Ma.

All this old fella did was, pick the wee boy up.

He smiled at the mother and she smiled back.

But the wee boy's face – Man, it lit up. It glowed, like the harvest moon; like the morning sun.

Arms. Welcoming arms. The good kind of arms. Maybe not as strong as they used to be, but strong enough.

He raises this wee laddie up and for the first time in weeks the wee face crinkles into laughter.

The man hoists him above his head and spins the wean round.

Around and around and around.

The boy's face is a thing to see. Eyes shining, looking up to the sky. Flying through the air. Sailing over the sea, the sand. Then looking down on his tired mammy, holding his wee arms out towards her.

Just some old guy. On a beach. In a different country.
A glimpse of another world.

Touches retirement letter
I've still got arms.
My heart's still beating, Ethel.
I feel as strong as I ever have…

Aye okay, in the morning I make the same noises as
a coffee machine.
And I'm aye dying for a pish. Minute I finish one it's
time for another.
Doesn't matter if I haven't even drank anything. It's
like my insides are turning to liquid.
Like I'm slowly melting.

There was just something… *uplifting* about that man
on the telly.
Is that me being sentimental again?
Transcendence. Getting o'er yourself.
I could be strong… If I wasn't always on the verge of
tears.

Beat.
(*As Ethel:*) Of course you are, Bob. We're all close to
tears now. Why shouldn't *you* be? How couldn't you
be?
You're in mourning…. Anger, despair, denial – they're
all stages of grief.
You could, if you wanted, keep right on digging that
grave of yours.
Let them lay you six feet under, stay there forever…

Giving up is easy. Surrender is so sweet. I've done my bit.

But it's useless.

Don't retreat, Bob. Don't let them drive you off the streets, make you scared of your neighbour. Scared of yourself.

Don't let them confine you.

Let the tears fall. Go on.

There's more than one way to be a man. All this Yes or No, Hard or Soft, Take It Like A Man, Big Boys don't Cry, No Fear... Of course you want to weep. Who wouldn't?

Doesn't mean your only choice is the opposite – from Woman-Hater to Man-Hater.

From being You, Bob, to being Me.

There was always plenty of confusion in me too – Don't go putting me on any pedestal. I gave up playing goddess –and demon – many moons ago.

Nothing is fixed, nothing permanent.

No jobs-for-life. No final answers. No one political theory. No *One* Bob Cunningham. No single Ethel. No final destination.

We're creatures of change. Gotta keep moving.

Forget about the questions, Bob. Live the answers.

A crash of – close – thunder.

All lights flicker. Then most go out.

Jaysus Fuddin' Murphy.

Scotland, eh? A thunderstorm, and the electricity goes on the blink.

Lights a candle

What? Is it the wrong kind of rain?

Me and Ethel, we saw this painting once. Cannae mind where.

It was of Judgement Day.

(Minister:) "And the land gave up its dead, and death and the grave gave up their dead! Death and the grave were thrown into the lake of fire!"

(Himself) But in this picture, people, ordinary people, were climbing back out of their graves. Throwing the lids off their coffins! Getting out and hugging each other, shaking hands.

I saw all of youse there. You, Eric, throwing your bunnet in the air. Polly, you were kissing your daughter. Bill, you're doing this mental wee dance.

Don't get me wrong – we were all wounded. Dirty and damp from the earth. No two ways about it, we'd been through the wars, all of us, clambering up out of our holes in the ground. But this wasn't a horror scene – it was joyous, preposterous, liberating!

A hectic, vivid, wild Necropolis. Waving and laughing, and scratching our heads, reading our own gravestones. "I wanna live again! Please, Clarence, let me live again!"

Ready to fight another day, do it all again.

And the gravediggers, they're standing there, watching all their hard labour being undone, lumps of earth and clay getting flung up and all of us climbing back out into the light.

And there am I, in the middle of this… mayhem, chaos, all the shouting and singing and confusion, trying to find Ethel. Everyone else is here. She must be too…

(Ethel:) Forget the questions, Bob. Don't look for me, not out here.
Remember the stories we used to tell.

(Himself:) Once upon a very deep time, there was
A man in a thunder storm....
Who flew to the top of a hill.

This is the night we stop mourning the dead.
Counting our losses. Regretting what we didn't achieve.
The dead are always with us. They're here. Now.
Like Jinnees. Jinns.
Join forces with them. That's what I say.
Don't lay down and die and hope for Paradise.
No – pull Heaven down here!
Throw a safety rope, a lifeline, up and lassoo the firmament - Heave, haul, pull, bring the dreams and the hopes down here!
Push, pull, haul, till we're covered in petals and stamens and confetti; smothered in golden dust.
In red, naked, leaves. In shooting stars.

We're ready for them –those mean, lonely, hollowed-out men who want to drag us down into their personal hell.
We're crawling out the graves they've dug for us. Up from under the crud and decay of greed and corruption and war. The sludge of defeats.
The would-be dictators. The erectors of fences and walls. The killers of children.
The old *aren't* costing the young – that's a vile distortion of the great gift of our fathers.

No, they're still at the same old game – dividing and ruling.
Sundering old from young, men from women, locals and immigrants, deplorables, politically correct...
But watch these new "leaders": they can't take dissent. They'll do anything to shut us up, close us down.
So – we refuse to disappear.
We refuse to go under.
Use all the revulsion and rage these narrow, deathly men and women fill you with, and stand your ground! Have faith, say when wrong is wrong. No embarrassment in standing strong for Love, Compassion, Indignation, Solidarity.
If we're falling – we're falling *upwards*.

Tears up retirement letter.
I don't know how long I've got. A week, a month, a decade. More, less.
Throws it over himself like confetti:
Stick your retirement up your arse!

Looks down at his feet:
Now we've climbed out our crypts, our tombs, the little boxes we built around ourselves, can't you feel it...?
That rocking under your feet.
Just a wee tremor. A shoogliness.
Can you hear the ground tearing, ripping?
We're moving up.
Feel it now? – the rock and roots cracking, the crust splitting.

We've stepped out of our graves.
We're standing.
Stand up.
Straight. Tall. Proud. Ready.
The only duty we have is – to *live*. To the last moment.
In whichever way that comes.
To resist. Keep on resisting.
Let's rise together.
"Yak-amár."
"Ya-rou-he."
We're on our feet. All of us. Strong together.
Our own wee common resurrection!
Sailing over the night, into the thunder.
This is our Ascension Day!

Thunder. Bob blows out the candle.